PARIS
THE CITY AT A GLANCE

D0245183

Palais de Chaillot
This monumental neoclassical co
facing the Eiffel Tower was built .
1937 International Exhibition.
Place du Trocadéro, 16ᵉ

Musée du quai Branly
Browse the collection of art from Africa,
Asia, Oceania and the Americas at this
museum designed by Jean Nouvel.
See p034

Centre Pompidou
You may need to make several trips to
the Centre Pompidou to take in all that it
has to offer, from world-class exhibitions
to iconic architecture.
See p014

Maison de Radio France
Discover the origins of French audio-visual
culture in the surprisingly good Radio France
museum housed here.
116 avenue du Président Kennedy, 16ᵉ,
T 5640 1516

Basilique du Sacré-Coeur
Even if you don't go inside, the ascent to
Sacré-Coeur is worth it for the views alone.
See p013

Institut du Monde Arabe
Middle Eastern motifs meet Jean Nouvel's
modern architecture in this striking building,
the best of Mitterand's *Grands Projets*.
1 rue des Fossés Saint-Bernard/Place
Mohammed V, 5ᵉ, T 4051 3838

Tour Montparnasse
Looming over low-rise Paris, this 210m-high
1975 landmark is back in fashion.
See p011

INTRODUCTION
THE CHANGING FACE OF THE URBAN SCENE

It is tempting to think that Paris never changes, that there is always a corner of the city where you really can catch a glimpse of Eugène de Rastignac or Jake Barnes, or stumble across a beatific Miles Davis en route to Club Saint-Germain, with a young Juliette Greco on his arm. But the truth is that Paris is a city of constant, if sometimes gentle, upheaval. Especially now. Ask any local who hops on their Vélib bicycle (see p032) to peddle across town to visit the Palais de Tokyo (13 avenue du Président Wilson, 16e, T 4723 5400) at 3am (part of the hugely popular Nuit Blanche scheme, when museums open all night for free). Or does lunch (whisper it), deli-style, at trendsetting bio-canteen Rose Bakery (see p033).

Not only is Paris now a more enjoyable place to be (largely thanks to initiatives by its mayor, Bertrand Delanoë), it's more relaxed. The *hauteur* has softened and the city brims with a new confidence. Yes, the past is alive in its *grandes dames* hotels, fashion flagships and Michelin-starred eateries, but many have undergone a contemporary redesign or simplified their cuisine. President Nicolas Sarkozy has a more ambitious vision, to reimagine the urban area entirely, creating a *Grand Paris* to rival London, Tokyo or New York. Ten architects – Jean Nouvel, Roland Castro, Richard Rogers and Winy Maas among them – have presented their plans at the Cité de l'Architecture et du Patronomie (1 place du Trocadéro, 16e, T 5851 5200). A new metropolis could be taking shape.

ESSENTIAL INFO
FACTS, FIGURES AND USEFUL ADDRESSES

TOURIST OFFICE
25 rue des Pyramides, 1er
T 08 9268 3000
parisinfo.com

TRANSPORT
Car hire
Avis
T 4862 5959
Metro
ratp.fr
Trains run from 5.20am to 1.20am
and until 2.20am on Saturday night
Taxis
Taxis G7
T 4739 4739

EMERGENCY SERVICES
Ambulance
T 15
Fire
T 18
Police
T 17
24-hour pharmacy
84 avenue des Champs-Élysées, 8e
T 4562 0241

EMBASSIES
British Embassy
18 rue d'Anjou, 8e
T 4451 3100
ukinfrance.fco.gov.uk
US Embassy
2 avenue Gabriel, 8e
T 4312 2222
france.usembassy.gov

MONEY
American Express
11 rue Scribe, 9e
T 4777 7000

POSTAL SERVICES
Post office
52 rue du Louvre, 1er
T 4028 2000
Shipping
UPS
T 08 2123 3877
ups.com

BOOKS
Inside Paris by Joe Friedman (Phaidon)
Paris 2000+: New Architecture by Sam
Lubell (Monacelli Press)
**The Flâneur: A Stroll Through the
Paradoxes of Paris** by Edmund White
(Bloomsbury)

WEBSITES
Art
louvre.fr
musee-orsay.fr
palaisdetokyo.com
Design
lesartsdecoratifs.fr
Newspapers
lejournaldudimanche.fr
lemonde.fr
Photography
mep-fr.org

COST OF LIVING
**Taxi from Charles de Gaulle Airport
to city centre**
€50
Cappuccino
€3
Packet of cigarettes
€6
Daily newspaper
€1.40
Bottle of champagne
€65

PARIS
Area
105 sq km
Population
2.2 million
Currency
Euro
Telephone codes
France: 33
Paris: 01
Time
GMT +1

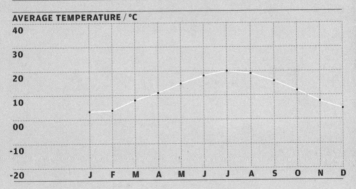

AVERAGE TEMPERATURE / °C

```
40

30

20

10

00

-10

-20    J  F  M  A  M  J  J  A  S  O  N  D
```

AVERAGE RAINFALL / MM

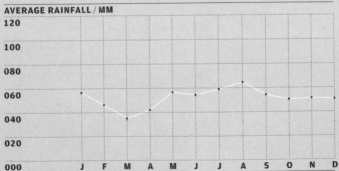

```
120

100

080

060

040

020

000    J  F  M  A  M  J  J  A  S  O  N  D
```

NEIGHBOURHOODS

THE AREAS YOU NEED TO KNOW AND WHY

To help you navigate the city, we've chosen the most interesting districts (see below and the map inside the back cover) and colour-coded our featured venues, according to their location; those venues that are outside these areas are not coloured.

MONTMARTRE

Rising above the city, Montmartre remains aloof from the rest of Paris. Check into the tranquil hideaway Hôtel Particulier (see p017) and explore the cafés and bars around rue des Trois Frères and rue des Abbesses, such as Café Burq (6 rue Burq). Have dinner at Guilo Guilo (see p042).

SAINT-MARTIN

It is alongside the banks of this canal that the east Paris bobo (bourgeois-bohème) crowd linger, weather permitting. Hip rue Beaurepaire is the epicentre. To the west is the trendy hangout La Fidélité (see p056). To the east, in the 19e, the bobos continue to push into Belleville.

GRANDS BOULEVARDS

There is a slight stain of tackiness around the Champs-Élysées itself, but the area still has plenty to offer, including the restaurant Senderens (see p046) and the fashionable Hôtel Plaza Athénée (see p028), where you should have a cocktail at the bar and book a treatment at the Dior Institut (see p089).

RÉPUBLIQUE AND BASTILLE

The best days of the legendary nightlife in the bars and clubs around rue Oberkampf might be a distant memory now, but there is no denying that the influx of BCBG (bon chic, bon genre) cash has helped the area scrub up nicely. Rue Paul Bert in Bastille is a gastro magnet and it's here you'll find one of our favourite eateries, Unico (see p041).

MARAIS

Made for the flâneur, the streets of the traditional Jewish quarter, centred around rue des Rosiers, rue Sainte-Croix de la Bretonnerie and rue Vieille-du-Temple, are peppered with cafés, galleries and one-off boutiques. On the district's eastern border is the fabulous Merci (see p037).

LOUVRE AND BEAUBOURG

The Louvre (place du Carrousel, T 4020 5050) is a must, for all its spirit-sapping bulk and Dan Brown-devouring hordes. Also visit the Musée des Arts Décoratifs (107 rue de Rivoli, T 4455 5760). Beaubourg combines art and Le Georges restaurant (T 4478 4799) in the Pompidou (see p014).

SAINT-GERMAIN AND QUARTIER LATIN

Still one of the chicest neighbourhoods in Paris – and home of swish department store Le Bon Marché (24 rue des Sèvres, T 4439 8000) – the heart of the Rive Gauche is packed with bookshops, cafés and, more recently, a clutch of art/design galleries, including Galerie Kreo (see p036).

LES INVALIDES

This area already comprised the largest collection of monuments in Paris. It now has another, in Jean Nouvel's Musée du quai Branly (see p034). Compare and contrast with the quarter's former architectural highpoint, the UNESCO HQ (see p012). Eat at Gaya (see p044) and L'Atelier de Joël Robuchon (see p054).

LANDMARKS

THE SHAPE OF THE CITY SKYLINE

Unlike Rome or Venice, Paris never has to live off its past for very long, because it always manages to reinvent itself. How it does this has a lot to do with the structure of the place. Paris has stuck to the same shape for centuries by spreading out steadily from the tiny island, now the Île de la Cité, where the Parisii, a community of Celtic fisherfolk, settled in 250BC. As its population grew, the city expanded outwards in concentric circles, stretching as far as the Périphérique ring road. Chloé-clad commuters lead *Desperate Housewives*-on-the-Seine lifestyles in the leafy western suburbs, such as Saint-Cloud and Neuilly, while the underclass re-enacts *La Haine* in 1950s hellholes north of the ring road.

Contemporary Paris consists of some two million people living inside the 9.7km diameter of the Périphérique, with the Île de la Cité still at its centre. The good news is that, while sprawling cities such as Los Angeles can afford to neglect their architecture, land is so precious within the unofficial boundary of Paris that Parisians strive to preserve theirs. And the city puts almost as much effort into building new monuments as it does into cherishing its old ones. Think of Henri IV ordering the construction of an expensive new residential district, the Marais, around Place des Vosges in the early 1600s. All of which means that not only is navigation easy in Paris, but the landmarks that line the way are worth lingering over. *For full addresses, see Resources.*

Grande Arche de la Défense

It was in the early 1950s that the proposal to construct a new business district to the west of Paris was first advanced, but it was only this 1989 landmark that fixed La Défense in the popular imagination. A hollowed cube standing 110m high, the stark, almost graphic lines of its façades are emphasised by the use of glazing and white Carrara marble. The creation of a Danish architect, Johan Otto von Spreckelsen, the arch is scaled on both sides by a pair of lifts, providing panoramic views of greater Paris, as well as down the axis of the Champs-Élysées. Nearby, the newest landmark in La Défense is French architect Christian de Portzamparc's angular granite tower for Groupe Société Générale, completed in 2008.

1 parvis de la Défense, T 4907 2755, grandearche.com

Tour Montparnasse

The redevelopment of the down-at-heel area around Gare Montparnasse in the early 1960s was, by and large, a piece of inspired city planning. Jean Dubuisson's scheme included a monumental slab of a residential block, with a wonderfully gridded curtain wall. Unfortunately, it also allowed for this 210m-high totem pole stuck in the middle of low-rise Paris. Together with other high-rise buildings along the Seine, which were commissioned under the prime ministership of Georges Pompidou, this tower, finished in 1973, has come back in vogue among city opinion-formers. There is an observation terrace and a bar on the 56th floor.

33 avenue du Maine, 15e, T 4538 5256,
www.tourmontparnasse56.com

UNESCO Headquarters

When this HQ complex was completed in 1958, writer Lewis Mumford dismissed it as a 'museum of antiquated modernities'. Even now, in the eyes of some critics, the building hasn't really recovered from this withering assessment. The work of a trio of celebrated architects, Marcel Breuer, Pier Luigi Nervi and Bernard Zehrfuss, it was one of the first major modern works to be built in the centre of the city. All the same, the seven-storey, Y-shaped office building, resting on 72 concrete stilts, has become a landmark. Breuer's congress hall, with its concertina-like concrete shells, has come to be seen as a masterpiece of modern design. The Japanese architect Tadao Ando added an exquisite small meditation space to the site, opened in 1995.

7 place de Fontenoy, 7ᵉ, unesco.org

Basilique du Sacré-Coeur

As navigational aids go, the Basilique du Sacré-Coeur, perched high above Montmartre, is hard to beat. The view it offers, back over Paris, is a tourist and postcard staple. But the church is altogether more surprising than that dreary status makes it seem. For a start, its Romano-Byzantine look is strictly repro. The creation of architect Paul Abadie, it was finished as recently as 1914.

In addition, it is one of the few churches ever built as a monument to failure, rather than in thanks for success. Specifically, it was created to help expiate the country's spiritual malaise; the main reason, it was thought, that France had received such a drubbing at the hands of Bismarck in the Franco-Prussian War.

35 rue du Chevalier-de-la-Barre, 18ᵉ, 1 5341 8900, sacre-coeur-montmartre.com

Centre Pompidou

The moment when architecture became icon can be traced squarely back to 1977, when Richard Rogers and Renzo Piano's technical and functional tour de force was unveiled to the world. One of the most visited buildings in France, it can seem a little untidy, but it is the classic example of a building as a city symbol. *Place Georges Pompidou, 4e, T 4478 1233, centrepompidou.fr*

HOTELS

WHERE TO STAY AND WHICH ROOMS TO BOOK

Paris is one of the world's great hotel cities, but nowhere, save perhaps New York, is the dissonance between palatial lobbies and sumptuous public rooms on the one hand, and bijou private spaces on the other, more jarring. Room selection is at least as important as the choice of hotel. You really need the cost/benefit analysis skills of a Nobel economist to work out the trade-off between a good room in a modest hotel and the reverse. We've highlighted the chicest *chambres* to help make that choice a little easier.

If you're yearning for old-school elegance, dust down those Hermès bags and check into the Plaza Athénée (see p028) or Le Meurice (228 rue de Rivoli, 1er, T 4458 1010). And what would Paris be without its idiosyncrasies? L'Hôtel (see p027) may be kitsch, but it is where Oscar Wilde languished while 'dying beyond his means'. Modern-day bohemians seeking art-inspired luxury should head to Hôtel Particulier (opposite). Among the more recent openings, we point you to Hôtel Fouquet's Barrière (46 avenue Georges V/avenue des Champs-Élysées, 8e, T 4069 6000), five buildings interlinked by architect Édouard François, with interiors by Jacques Garcia, and the Roland Castro/Philippe Starck-designed Mama Shelter (see p023), in the edgy 20e arrondissement to the east. Due to open in 2010 is another Starck project, the reimagined Royal Monceau (37 avenue Hoche, 8e, T 4299 8800). *For full addresses and room rates, see Resources.*

Hôtel Particulier

Despite the swarms of tourists en route to Sacré-Coeur (see p013), and a decade of slow but steady gentrification, pockets of Montmartre retain an atmosphere unmatched anywhere else in Paris. Head north of place des Abbesses, and just off the stylish avenue Junot you'll find the discreetly situated Hôtel Particulier, a 19th-century townhouse once owned by the Hermès family, set in private gardens created by landscaper Louis Benéch. Film-maker Morgane Rousseau transformed the property into a five-suite hotel in 2007, inviting five Parisian artists to design a room each; Natacha Lesueur's Curtain of Hair Suite (overleaf). Finnish interior designer Mats Haglund was responsible for the exquisitely furnished salon.

23 avenue Junot, 18e, T 5341 8140, hotel-particulier-montmartre.com

Hôtel du Petit Moulin

Tucked away in the Marais, not far from
the Musée Picasso (T 4271 2521), the façade
of this former *boulangerie*, where Victor
Hugo once bought his bread (though Hugo
crops up with suspicious regularity in
Paris sales-speak), has remained
untouched. In the reception area of the
hotel, which opened in 2005, original
timbered ceilings complement leather
sofas, shimmering fabrics, colourful
ceramic tables and illustrations by the
Petit Moulin's creator, Christian Lacroix.
Inside the lift, the theatrical rococo décor
sets the scene for the 17 individually
designed guest rooms. Quirky wallpapers
and glamorous textiles, from velour to
fur, Venetian mirrors and mosaic-tiled
bathrooms, all help to create a different
ambience in each, from rustic to pop.
We particularly like Room 204 (above).
29-31 rue du Poitou, 3e, T 4274 1010,
paris-hotel-petitmoulin.com

9 Hotel

At the chic and cheerful end of the boutique spectrum, the three-star 9 Hotel was remodelled in 2007 by Barcelona's Castell Veciana design studio into an uncluttered, functional and business-like space with 35 rooms spread over six floors. The traditional façade and historic surroundings hide a very pleasing modern monochrome interior with ebony parquet floors. We especially liked the whitewashed stone cave that is the breakfast/dining room. Some of the standard rooms can be pokey, so ask for one of the seven Superior Rooms. The location, close to Gare de l'Est and Gare du Nord, make this hotel ideal for a weekend visit.
14 rue Papillon, 9e, T 4770 7834, le9hotel.com

Mama Shelter

It may be a schlep from the centre (about 15 minutes on Ligne 3 from Gambetta), but this is one of the hottest places to stay in town right now. And the gritty location, in the graffiti-ridden *quartier* of Saint-Blaise, is the point. Mama Shelter opened in 2008, and was conceived as a hotel-cum-urban retreat by Serge Trigano, Cyril Aouizerate, Philippe Starck and Roland Castro. Carved out of a former multistorey car park, the 172-room property is full of witty Starckisms, such as the mask lights in the rooms (overleaf) and tree-trunk stools in the lobby (above), and offers lots of opportunities for hanging out (there's no room service) in the lobby, bar and restaurant headed by Alain Senderens. It's hip and definitely worth the hike.
109 rue de Bagnolet, 20ᵉ, T 4348 4848, mamashelter.com

Hôtel Le A

'This place is not to sleep, it is to dream,' says artist Fabrice Hyber, who, together with interior architect Frédéric Mechiche, created this unique ensemble of practical comfort and artistic vision, close to the Champs-Élysées. The massive tapestries in the entrance, the wall paintings that continue from the inside to the hotel's exterior, and even the room number plates are all Hyber's work. The large black-and-white lounge area (above) is divided into a bar and an art-book-stuffed library, while the 25 rooms and one apartment are supposed to correspond to the letters of the alphabet. If you like to wash *à la japonaise,* reserve Junior Suite 402, which is one of five with a bath and a separate shower.
4 rue d'Artois, 8ᵉ, T 4256 9999, paris-hotel-a.com

L'Hôtel

This former *pavilion d'amour* was built in the 19th century, when Saint-Germain boasted a large park used by the French aristocracy – and all that fresh air evidently encouraged fervid thoughts of exercising their collective *droit de seigneur*. Interior designer Jacques Garcia was responsible for the redecoration, in 2001, of the 20 highly individual rooms. Our favourite is the art deco Room 36, which was the stripper Mistinguett's choice, while Oscar Wilde expired amid the splendid Victoriana of Room 16 (above). *13 rue des Beaux Arts, 6e, T 4441 9900, l-hotel.com*

Hôtel Plaza Athénée

Opened in 1911, this sumptuous hotel has been given a 21st-century redecoration. Executive chef Alain Ducasse and Paris-based interior designer Patrick Jouin teamed up to effect the transformation, and in the process made the restaurant, and especially the bar, among the city's most talked-about places. The rooms are a mixed bag. On the fifth floor, the Royal Suite boasts 450 sq m and a partial view of the Eiffel Tower, but the style is more than a little fussy. The Deluxe Rooms are a better bet. The Terrasse Montaigne (T 5367 6600) is the place to be seen, while La Cour Jardin (above) is preferable if you'd rather do the watching yourself. For some beautifying beforehand, book a treatment at the in-house Dior Institut (see p089). *25 avenue Montaigne, 8ᵉ, T 5367 6665, www.plaza-athenee-paris.com*

Le Bellechasse

Remodelled in 2007 by Christian Lacroix, the 34-room Le Bellechasse is not a reservation for fans of minimalism or 15 shades of grey. The rooms are riotous in their décor, to say the least – all giant sun faces, peacocks, Victorian gentlemen with butterfly wings and bold blocks of colour, not to mention the faux alligator-skin tiling in the bathrooms. And yet, in an over-the-top way, the baroque approach mixed with a few contemporary touches (some plain concrete walls and odd pieces of furniture) works. If Starck produces hotel as urban theatre, this is boutique hotel as grand pantomime dame. We like the Quai d'Orsay Rooms (above). Le Bellechasse is minutes from the Musée d'Orsay on rue de Lille (T 4049 4814).
8 rue de Bellechasse, 7ᵉ, T 4550 2231, lebellechasse.com

3 Rooms

After creating the Milan jewel 10 Corso Como, Carla Sozzani got together with Tunisian fashion designer Azzedine Alaïa to open a small hotel in the Marais. The three apartments are a study in understated perfection. Alaïa donated furniture from his private collection, including chairs by Marc Newson and tables by Jean Prouvé.

7 rue de Moussy, 4ᵉ, T 4478 9200

24 HOURS

SEE THE BEST OF THE CITY IN JUST ONE DAY

We all have our own fantasies of the perfect Parisian day. Does there, for instance, really seem any better way to lead an adult life than to scribble a few iconoclastic insights into the human condition over a café au lait at Café de Flore (172 boulevard Saint-Germain, 5ᵉ, T 4548 5526), then dash off to an early-evening screening of Robert Bresson's *Pickpocket*, before spending what is left of the night listening to jazz, and afterwards seducing either Arthur Koestler or Simone de Beauvoir, according to taste?

Okay, so the golden age of the existentialists has been exposed by the revisionists. Sartre was simply a satyr who got lucky, and de Beauvoir was a manipulative minx who couldn't hold her drink and made up her memoirs. But the point is that nothing can shake our faith in Paris. Our ideal day there will always differ, but, right now, we'd start with peddling around on one of the many Vélib rental bikes (opposite) that you can pick up from racks located around the city (T 3079 7930, velib.paris.fr). Devote the day to exceptional design, taking in Jean Nouvel's Musée de quai Branly (overleaf), where the restaurant Les Ombres (T 4753 6800) makes a great stop for lunch with a view, and Galerie Kreo (see p036). Later on, mooch around the Marais, stopping for coffee at concept-cum-vintage store Merci (see p037). Have dinner on the Left Bank at La Société (see p038), lingering until late to listen to live jazz. *For full addresses, see Resources.*

10.30 Breakfast

The French don't really 'do' big breakfasts, so your choice of venue in Paris will be more geographical than gourmet. Choose a see-and-be-seen *terrasse* to park your Vélib, and order a café au lait and croissant while you map out the day. Café Charlot (T 4454 0330) and La Perle (T 4272 6993) in the Marais; Chez Jeannette (T 4770 3089) in the 10e; Café Marly (T 4926 0660), facing IM Pei's Louvre pyramid; and Le Bar du Marché (T 4326 5515) in Saint-Germain are some of our haunts. For a swish start, try La Galerie at Hôtel Georges V (T 4952 7006). Alternatively, get ready to pump those pedals with some energising eco food from Rose Bakery, which has branches in the 9e (T 4282 1280) and the 3e (T 4996 5401), or a rich hot chocolate at the charmingly shabby Angelina (T 4260 8200) on rue de Rivoli.

12.00 Musée du quai Branly
In 2008, French architect Jean Nouvel finally picked up his Pritzker. It was, according to many, long overdue, though Nouvel's long-time friend Frank Gehry was quick to offer an explanation. Unlike Zaha Hadid, or Gehry indeed, Nouvel has nothing you could call a signature style. His projects are site-specific – genuine attempts to create unique buildings. It was the Institut du Monde Arabe (T 4051 3838), opened in 1987 in Paris, that made the architect a star. After that came the Fondation Cartier (T 4218 5650) in 1994, and Musée du Quai Branly in 2006, which is where we suggest you begin your Nouvel tour. Showing non-Western art, the building looks like a long footbridge set amid a forest of green, and is protected from the traffic on quai Branly by a glass screen. One wall is covered by Patrick Blanc's 'vertical garden'. *37 quai Branly, 7ᵉ, T 5661 7172, quaibranly.fr*

15.00 Galerie Kreo

Since launching Kreo in 1999, Clémence and Didier Krzentowski have, true to the Esperanto translation of the gallery's name, 'created' extensively. They have a remarkably fluid ethos when it comes to the designers with whom they work, accepting that development takes time and costs money. But these factors don't hinder them in their quest to produce the finest limited-edition furniture and lighting. Over the years, the couple have built up a tightly edited pool of designers, from Jasper Morrison to Wieki Somers. Pictured are Marc Newson's 'Carbon' ladder, Pierre Charpin's 'Lune' mirror, and Ronan and Erwan Bouroullec's 'Geta' table.
31 rue Dauphine, 6ᵉ, T 5310 2300
galeriekreo.com

16.30 Merci

Three decades after creating Bonpoint, the ultimate fashion destination for pint-sized patricians, Marie-France and Bernard Cohen began all over again with Merci, a concept store in the upper Marais. Housed in an 1840 building that was once a factory for textile company Braquenié, it's a place where you can find a copy of Gide's *L'Immortaliste*, a Cappellini sofa, an Opinel pocket knife or a Dries Van Noten jacket. Cheap sits next to *cher*. The project is as ambitious as 10 Corso Como or The Conran Shop were back in the day, but with a difference – all the profits go to charity. Order an espresso and browse the 10,000 or so secondhand titles (there's a section of English editions) in the bookshop/café (above).
*111 boulevard Beaumarchais, 3ᵉ,
T 4277 0033*

20.00 La Société

Nestled in the ample artistic bosom of
Saint-Germain-des-Prés, La Société is
an expansive restaurant that combines
dense British oakiness with a flurry of
Parisian airiness. Owners Jean-Louis
Costes and Alex Denis opted for classic
over contemporary, with a sophisticated
chocolate-brown interior by Parisian
design stalwart Christian Liaigre, featuring
some custom-made pieces. Art adds to
the refined opulence, with photographs
by Peter Lindbergh, a white marble
champagne bar by Sophie Lafont and
sculptures by Mathieu Lévy and Sara
Favriau. Opened in March 2008, the
restaurant can seat up to 120, and the
menu is French brasserie cuisine.
La Société also puts on a programme
of live music (Sundays and Mondays).
4 place Saint-Germain, 6ᵉ, T 5363 6060

URBAN LIFE

CAFÉS, RESTAURANTS, BARS AND NIGHTCLUBS

Eating out in Paris is a more relaxed affair these days, though it's perhaps comforting to know that your waiter may still be horrified if you ask for milk in your espresso or butter with your croissant. Food-savvy Parisians will cross the city for an exceptional meal, and the most sought-after *tables gastronomiques* right now are the Franco-Asian hybrids. Guilo Guilo (overleaf) is among those leading the trend, while bold set menus from chefs such as Peter Nilsson at La Gazzetta (29 rue de Cotte, 12e, T 4347 4705) reflect Nordic and Japanese influences in *la bistronomie* – the French equivalent of the gastropub. There's also a new wave of produce-driven bistro/wine bars, such as Glou (101 rue Vieille-du-Temple, 3e, T 4274 4432) and Racines (8 passage des Panoramas, 2e, T 4013 0641), popping up, following in the footsteps of the forerunner, Rose Bakery (see p033), which now has two branches in the city. If you hanker for classic Parisian elegance, try Apicius (see p055), 1728 (8 rue d'Anjou, 8e, T 4017 0477) or Senderens (see p046).

The after-hours scene keeps getting better. The irrepressible Costes clan continue to add to their portfolio, while artist-entrepreneur André Saraiva, who is behind hip *boîte* Le Baron (6 avenue Marceau, 8e, T 4720 0401), has created a *branché* hangout at La Fidélité (see p056), and also resuscitated several dying clubs, including Le Régine (49-51 rue de Ponthieu, 8e, T 4359 2113). *For full addresses, see Resources.*

Unico

Rue Paul Bert in the 11ᵉ is the city's culinary golden mile. Le Bistrot Paul Bert (T 4372 2401), adored by chefs and critics alike, and its seafood sister L'Ecailler du Bistrot (T 4372 7677) can come to the rescue if Unico is full. And it may very well be, as it has hardly emptied since Argentines Marcelo Joulia and Enrique Zanoni lugged a charcoal-burning stove from deep in the pampas and installed it in the kitchen of this former butcher's shop in 2006. The original orange 1970s décor was largely left alone, and played up with pop colours, patterned walls and vintage furniture, including a communal table designed by Norman Foster. The service is earnest and energetic, and the Argentine steak and *empanadas* the best in Paris.
15 rue Paul Bert, 11ᵉ, T 4367 6808, resto-unico.com

Guilo Guilo
This micro-bistro set Paris alight when
it opened in 2008. The 10-course tasting
menu is served as simultaneously as chef
Eiichi Edakuni from Kyoto and his two
aides can manage – a true performance
for the 20-odd diners seated around the
high black bar and in the adjacent private
salon, designed by Christophe Pillet.
8 rue Garreau, 18ᵉ, T 4254 2392,
guiloguilo.com

Gaya Rive Gauche

Christian Ghion's redesign of what was a famously hideous space signalled a fresh approach to chef Pierre Gagnaire's always interesting food. Gagnaire took over this restaurant, in the heart of Saint-Germain, i 2005, and the décor was hailed a success for its light touch and contemporary edge – the perfect match for Gagnaire's forward-thinking cooking. The menu here is dedicated to fish and seafood, featuring dishes that exemplify the chef's signature style – intricate combinations of taste and texture. The restaurant was awarded a Michelin star in 2006. Book well in advance, and if you can't get a table, have a glass of wine at the bar. Closed Sundays. Gagnaire's eponymous three-starred restaurant is on rue Balzac (T 5836 1250). *44 rue du Bac, 7ᵉ, T 4544 7373, pierre-gagnaire.com*

Senderens

In 2005, Alain Senderens, then head chef at the three-Michelin-starred restaurant Lucas Carton, calmly gave up his stars and changed direction. He reopened at the same address later that year, renaming his caterie Senderens, and presenting a new menu and relatively economical prices. Senderens' cooking, awarded two Michelin stars here in 2006, remains an immaculate fusion of local and global ingredients and flavours, though everything about the experience at this restaurant is less stuffy and rarified than before. The space was designed by Noé Duchaufour-Lawrance, whose muted palette blends beautifully with the original art nouveau interior of this listed building in Madeleine.
9 place de la Madeleine, 8ᵉ, T 4265 2290, senderens.fr

Benoit

Situated close to the Centre Pompidou (see p014), Benoit has been serving traditional French food since 1912. It is perhaps a little too popular with visitors, but if that's a fault, it's one now shared by almost every good restaurant in Paris. Michel Petit, whose family had been the owners for three generations, sold the concern to Alain Ducasse in 2005, who extended the franchise with an outpost in Tokyo. Benoit is like the Platonic ideal of the perfect Parisian brasserie. Portions are generous and the cooking is consistent; the restaurant has one Michelin star. This isn't the place to unveil the vintage Chanel suit you just picked up in Didier Ludot (T 4296 0656), but sometimes everyone needs a night off from the *beau monde*. *20 rue Saint-Martin, 4ᵉ, T 4272 2576, benoit-paris.*

Cristal Room, Baccarat

As you can imagine, the waiting list for the Cristal Room restaurant stretches as far as the fabulous 13m-long Philippe Starck-designed table in the Maison Baccarat boutique; the wait is even longer for the nine-seater Pink Salon private room. The building, which includes this restaurant on the first floor, was originally built for art patron Marie-Laure de Noailles. Original chandeliers hang alongside modern pieces by designers such as Yves Savinel and Gilles Rozé. Together with the flawless crystal glass and plethora of mirrors, it all creates a stunning display of refracted light. Chef Thomas L'Hérisson (with Guy Martin as consultant) presents a superbly executed menu of traditional French cuisine with a few interesting twists.
11 place des États-Unis, 16ᵉ, T 4022 1110, baccarat.com

Le Cochon à l'Oreille
One of the most beautifully ornate bistro/brasseries in Paris, Le Cochon is small (there are only 15 or so covers) but perfectly formed. The tiles covering the walls depict market scenes from an era when Les Halles was truly 'the belly of Paris'. The classic brasserie fare of crudités, charcuterie and steak frites is simple and honest.
15 rue Montmartre, 1er. T 4236 0756

Les HALLES apres le
COUP de CLOCHE

Germain

One of the more recent openings in the Costes empire's steady takeover of some of the best locations in Paris, Germain replaces L'Arbuci, a tired let's-eat-and-get-it-over-with brasserie. And it's a welcome addition on this busy street, which is missing a place or two with a lounge/club vibe. India Mahdavi's décor, and 'Sophie', the yellow statue created by French artist Xavier Veilhan, may not appeal to everyone, but they certainly give the space an energy, which spreads (noisily) through the different areas: the ground-floor café (right) and upstairs in the more intimate lounge. The menu is dinerish, with a couple of nice surprises in the fish and chips and excellent steaks. It ain't cheap, but then the food isn't really what you are paying for in this bastion of *branchitude*. Service is cheerful, but the door policy at weekends is ruthless.
25-27 rue de Buci, 6ᵉ, T 4326 0293

L'Atelier de Joël Robuchon

There have been many attempts at reinvention by Parisian chefs concerned that the market for creamy, formal French cuisine is dying off. L'Atelier is just about the best example. Here, Joël Robuchon offers haute cuisine served in petite, tapas-style portions. Diners sit around a bar area, overlooking an open kitchen. The stretch limos parked outside tell you all you need to know about the calibre of the clientele. The restaurant currently holds two Michelin stars, and the no-reservation rule has been relaxed a little: you can book seating before 12.30pm (service starts at 11.30am) or at 6.30pm.
5 rue Montalembert, 7ᵉ, T 4222 5656, joel-robuchon.com

Apicius

Almost everything you read about Apicius makes Jean-Pierre Vigato's temple to fine dining sound faintly ridiculous. His use of Heinz tomato ketchup in delicate fish dishes, for instance, or the overpowering sweet-and-sour sauce he makes for the finest, most delicate foie gras. In short, none of it should work; in practice, almost all of it does. If there is a fault, it is that we are solidly in gastro-tourism territory here, and the clientele can lean away from the glamorous and solidly in the direction of the over-earnest, although the room offers the necessary sense of occasion, and the food really is sensational enough to convert even the terminally jaded. Closed weekends and throughout August. *20 rue d'Artois, 8ᵉ, T 4380 1966*

La Fidélité

Tucked in a rather unexciting corner of the 10ᵉ, La Fidélité is a big, easy space, with a feel somewhere between a French brasserie and a Viennese coffee house, with its creamy colours, high ceilings and mirrored walls. The food is copious, tasty and (at lunchtime) pretty good value, though it's at night and in the lounge area downstairs (above) that the place really comes alive. Opened in December 2008 by André Saraiva and Lionel Bensemoun, La Fidélité was swiftly adopted by the in-crowd, although the atmosphere has remained lazily intimate and sexily discreet – exactly the kind of place that Paris is so good at creating.
12 rue de la Fidélité, 10ᵉ, T 4770 1934

The Ritz Bar

When César Ritz opened The Ritz hotel in 1898, it had plenty of glittering chandeliers and luxurious rooms but no bar. The Cambon arrived in 1921, when it became the meeting point of *le tout Paris*. In 1936, César's daughter-in-law, Monique, entered the men-only club and declared it open to women; Coco Chanel quickly became a regular. Now the bar has been renamed, given a plush refurbishment and has installed hot resident DJs, it's once again hosting glitzy soirées. Order a Ritz 75, the mandarin-and-champagne house cocktail, and soak up the opulent surrounds – the red marble fireplace, the giant 'tree' adorned with Portieux crystal glasses and walls covered with 'Noir Amour' fabric designed by Clara Lander. Open Wednesday to Saturday until 2am.
38 rue Cambon, 1er, T 4316 3030

Ladurée Le Bar

Located at the back of Ladurée's Champs-Élysées branch, Le Bar is a flamboyant contemporary foil to the Jacques Garcia-designed tea room at the front. Opened in 1997, the original *salon de thé* is showing its age, which makes this a far more glamorous perch for a coffee or post-shopping cocktail. With a dramatic resin bar and cobweb-like detailing, interior designer Roxane Rodriguez has created a space full of sinuous curves. Head chef Michel Lerout offers up a menu of light, savoury dishes, while Philippe Andrieu delivers suitably sophisticated pâtisserie. If you're in search of Ladurée's legendary *macarons*, we suggest you do like a local and buy them at the rue Royale branch (T 4260 2179) in the 8e.
13 rue Lincoln, 8e, T 4075 0875, laduree.com

Paris Social Club
Designed by French collective EXYZT, the
former Triptyque was transformed into
this seriously respected DJ venue in 2008.
It has built a reputation as one of the best
clubs in town, where dedicated electro,
rap and punk fans flock to the dancefloor.
Entrance is free or about €7 midweek;
€15 for a big name at the weekend.
142 rue Montmartre, 2ᵉ, T 4028 0555,
parissocialclub.com

INSIDERS' GUIDE
VANESSA AND LAETITIA ROGGWILLER, BOUTIQUE OWNERS

Born in the 16e arrondissement, sisters Vanessa and Laetitia Roggwiller are passionate about their hometown – its architecture, its culture and, of course, its fashion. In 2009, they opened concept store Hôtel Particulier (see p078) in Montorgeuil, an area Vanessa describes as a 'trendy village in the heart of the city'.

When friends drop by on a Saturday, Vanessa (opposite, on left) breaks for lunch at Le Café (62 rue Tiquetonne, 2e, T 4039 0800), while Laetitia (on right) is a regular at Au Rocher de Cancale (78 rue Montorgeuil, 2e, T 4233 5029), where the convivial atmosphere and *salade sud* with spiced tuna keep her coming back. For a relaxed Sunday brunch, the 'cosy' Le Fumoir (6 rue de l'Amiral de Coligny, 1er, T 4292 0024), facing the Louvre, is Laetitia's top spot, while her sister prefers the hip Murano Urban Resort (13 boulevard du Temple, 3e, T 4271 2000), which in her opinion 'serves the best brunch in town'. After work, for an *apéro chic*, Vanessa is a fan of the bar at Pershing Hall (49 rue Pierre Charron, 8e, T 5836 5800), for its 'great cocktails and intimate ambience'. Laetitia heads to Pigalle and the *décalé* Hôtel Amour (8 rue Navarin, 9e, T 4878 3180).

After hours, Vanessa dances until the early hours at the super-stylish Chacha Club (47 rue Berger, 1er, T 4013 1212), while her sister makes for Montmartre, and the chilled-out cocktail lounge at the Kube hotel (1-5 passage Ruelle, 18e, T 4205 2000).

For full addresses, see Resources.

ARCHITOUR
A GUIDE TO THE CITY'S ICONIC BUILDINGS

There are a dozen Le Corbusier buildings in and around Paris, the city where he lived and worked for most of his adult life. Today, some, such as Villa Besnus (85 boulevard de la République), the family home completed in 1922 in the suburb of Vaucresson, are almost unrecognisable. Others, such as the 1951 Maisons Jaoul (83 rue de Longchamp, 16e) in leafy Neuilly-sur-Seine, which was a gossip-magazine staple when it belonged to Lord Palumbo and served as a base for his friends, including the late Princess Diana, have been carefully restored. But most of Le Corbusier's projects in Paris are concentrated into a crescent across the southern half of the city, and can be squeezed into half a day's architourism, or combined, as we suggest, with a selection of other modern gems.

Cité de Refuge (opposite) is a good starting point, while just a few streets away is Maison Planeix (24 boulevard Masséna, 13e). A house-cum-studio, it was designed for one of Le Corbusier's most ardent, if impecunious, clients, the sculptor Antonin Planeix. The Atelier Ozenfant (53 avenue Reille, 14e) is another live/work space by the architect. By the early 1930s, Le Corbu was back in the 14e for his first public commission, the Pavillon Suisse. He revisited the site for Maison du Brésil in 1959 (see p068). The Fondation Le Corbusier (8-10 square du Docteur Blanche, 16e, T 4288 4153; closed Sundays and Monday morning) can advise on visits.
For full addresses, see Resources.

Cité de Refuge

Located on dusty rue Cantagrel, Cité de Refuge was built as a Salvation Army hostel in 1933. Le Corbusier conceived it as a ship, with the entrance hall as the deck and numerous floors of cabin-style accommodation looming above. The signature sheer, double-glazed curtain wall was actually the source of many of the building's problems. The experimental double glazing never really worked as well as intended, and the place became notorious as an oven in the summer and a freezer in winter. Because of this, the building helped Le Corbusier rethink the nature of the free façade and how to make better use of his famous brise-soleil.

12 rue Cantagrel, 13ᵉ

Sanofi-Aventis building

Although Jean-Pierre Buffi worked with Jean Prouvé, the architect is best known now for a series of offices that can seem understated to the point of anonymity. Yet the pharmaceutical giant that commissioned this building on the Seine got his best work. It doesn't reach the heights of the company's former home, Tour Initiale, but it cuts a dash at night.
42-50 quai de la Rapée, 12ᵉ

Maison du Brésil

While the Pavillon Suisse formed the first step in Le Corbusier's development of the Cité Radieuse – his ideal of communal living – it was this 1959 building that helped seriously curtail, if not end, its scope. Intended as a hostel for Brazilian students, and executed as a replica of the Cité Radieuse apartment block in Marseille, this Parisian project was intended to prove that the same architectural formula would work in any climate. Unfortunately, the theory didn't withstand the reality of Parisian winters, and the concrete façade is now scarred by age and pollution. Maison du Brésil stands as an admittedly tarnished testament to the time when we all believed that architecture could change the world.
7L boulevard Jourdan, 14ᵉ, T 5810 2300, maisondubresil.org

Maison de Verre

One of the greatest houses built in the International Style is also one of the least visited. Architects Pierre Chareau and Bernard Bijvoet worked wonders on the foundations of an existing building in a small plot in the 7ᵉ, completing the new structure in 1932. The façades are covered with glass blocks set into a steel frame, which creates a well of light while ensuring privacy. The double-height living room is the real show-stopper, one wall of which is covered with a sliding-panel bookcase, and features adjustable louvres, exposed bolts and thin slabs of slate attached to the piers. Wires were threaded through the metal tubing that runs from floor to ceiling. Visits must be arranged in advance in writing, but it is possible to glimpse the house from the outside.
31 rue Saint-Guillaume, 7ᵉ

Boulogne-Billancourt

Unless there is a special place in your heart reserved for hotbeds of 1960s radicalism, it is unlikely that the grimy, still rather edgy, *banlieue* Boulogne-Billancourt will have featured heavily in your trips to Paris. But the site of the Renault strikes of the 1960s is a surprisingly good place to search out overlooked architectural gems, such as Le Corbusier's early Maison Cook, the Collinet house by Robert Mallet-Stevens and the liner-like apartments built by Georges-Henri Pingusson in 1936, all located on rue Denfert-Rochereau. While these buildings take some tracking down, it is impossible to miss the suburb's more recent claim to architectural fame – the mid-1970s city of apartments (pictured), by Daniel Badani, Pierre Roux-Dorlut and Pierre Vigneron, which has reshaped the skyline along rue de Vieux Pont de Sèvres.

SHOPPING

THE BEST RETAIL THERAPY AND WHAT TO BUY

Shoppers in Paris are split between a historical fascination with the city as the home of some of the greatest fashion, beauty and design institutions on the planet, and a desire to seek out the fresh new purveyors of its legendary style. The Right Bank is still dominated by the old establishments – Goyard (352 rue Saint-Honoré, 1er, T 5504 7260), Lanvin (15 and 22 rue du Faubourg Saint-Honoré, 8e, T 4471 3125/4471 3173) and Pierre Cardin (59 rue du Faubourg Saint-Honoré, 8e, T 4266 9225) are essential stops – but it's also home now to contemporary arrivals in French fashion, like Mary Beyer (opposite) in the modish Palais-Royal.

Make your way east to the 3e and 4e arrondissements and you will arrive in the maze-like Marais, where Azzedine Alaïa (see p080) has a shop, alongside lots of interesting boutique/galleries such as Le Petit Endroit (14 rue Portefoin, 3e, T 4233 9318) and ToolsGalerie (119 rue Vieille-du-Temple, 3e, T 4277 3580), which shows mostly up-and-coming designers. Continue your design tour on the edge of the Marais at Patrick Seguin (see p081), before crossing over to the Left Bank, where Saint-Germain is rapidly becoming a hotbed of high-calibre art/design showrooms. We recommend beginning at Perimeter Editions (47 rue Saint-André-des-Arts, 6e, T 5542 0122), Cat-Berro (25 rue Guénégaud, 6e, T 4325 5810) and the pioneering Galerie Kreo (see p036).

For full addresses, see Resources.

Mary Beyer

The Palais-Royal arcades (Galerie Valois and Galerie Montpensier) are shoppers' jewels – centrally located and neatly concealing a clutch of chic addresses. One of our favourite boutiques is the eponymous label of former YSL model Mary Beyer, who turned her hand to gloves in 2000 after buying venerable French glove-making company Lavabre Cadet. Since then, her designs have been a huge hit and she has supplied the likes of Chanel and Alaïa (see p080). More recently, she has created collections for Balenciaga and Stéphane Rolland. Beyer works mostly in kid ('Printemps' men's glove, €410, above), which she combines with ostrich, mink and crocodile. Her made-to-measure service takes 15 days. *32-33 Galerie Montpensier, 1er, T 4261 4185, marybeyer.com*

Pierre Hardy
One of the early arrivals in the Palais-Royal, in 2003, Pierre Hardy opened a second boutique over on the Left Bank (right) in February 2009 – a dark and seductive showcase for his edgy shoes and accessories. The floor and ceiling of the 50 sq m space, designed in conjunction with BP Architectures, are covered in black waxed linoleum. The only natural light is provided by the large glass frontage, and an illuminated Plexiglas 'lightbox', for which Hardy creates different artwork for each new collection, dissects the space. Prior to launching his own label in 1999, Hardy designed footwear for Dior, Hermès and Balenciaga. Currently, he also produces limited-edition lines for Gap and Kitsuné.
9-11 place du Palais Bourbon, 7e,
T 4555 0067, pierrehardy.com

Pierre Hermé

French pastry chef Pierre Hermé hired a Belgian architect, Olivier Lempereur, to design his first Right Bank address, opened in 2008 on rue Cambon. The result is an enticing little store, all curves and squares like the delicacies inside. A glass door slides open in the chocolate-brown façade, revealing gently concave walls of the same colour, stamped with squares to look like chocolate bars. Above, multicoloured panels cover the lights like iridescent fruit jellies. Customers queue at a store-length counter to buy *macarons* in adventurous flavours, such as caramel with *fleur de sel*, grapefruit with wasabi, or peach, apricot and saffron. O-shaped boxes each holding two dozen of the chewy little pastries make the best hostess gift in town.
4 rue Cambon, 1er, T 4354 4777,
pierreherme.com

Pinel & Pinel

Fred Pinel is the kind of luggage designer who would have done Waugh's William Boot proud. The fictitious war reporter hit Abyssinia with more than 200kg of luggage, including a canoe. Pinel & Pinel could make a leather trunk for it in a choice of 51 colours. Its more up-to-date range includes the 'I-Trunk', containing a 20in iMac, Canon printer and JBL speakers. Other items in the line hold a home cinema, a music system and a Brompton folding bike (above). The sublimely ridiculous 'Pic Nic' trunk carries Krug champagne, a Thermos flask and a truffle slicer. It also weighs 60kg, so make sure there is someone around to carry it into a field for you. You can also have bespoke trunks made to fit your exact whim.
5 rue Cyrano de Bergerac, 18e, T 4523 1114, pineletpinel.com

Hôtel Particulier

Conceptual retailing has been de rigueur since Colette took Paris by storm in 1997. Newcomer Hôtel Particulier, opened in March 2009, is the brainchild of the Roggwiller sisters, Vanessa and Laetitia (see p062), and is set in an 18th-century mansion modernised by Antwerp-based architect Dirk Engelen, who installed black and white wood strips on the walls and black parquet flooring. As for the contents, the emphasis is on fashion, and a mix of well-known names (Jean-Charles de Castelbajac, Kris Van Assche, Gaspard Yurkievich) and new talent. Look for the baroque-inspired offerings from Japanese brand Dress 33 and silk-screened tees by Gilles & Maurice. Everything else is for sale too, from accessories to furniture.
15 rue Léopold Bellan, 2e, T 4039 9000, hotelparticulier-paris.com

Azzedine Alaïa

This circular shop, with interior walls covered in pale Carrara marble, is the most recent addition to Alaïa's Paris headquarters. Designed by Marc Newson with architect Sébastien Segers, it is a shrine to the Tunisian-born designer's shoes and accessories, which are displayed in alcoves lined with pale leather, rather like museum pieces. Café au lait-coloured leather cushions cover a bench that surrounds a distinctly palatial central column, softening the austere effect of the marble and giving the whole space a supremely elegant look. Clothes are presented in a separate area.
7 rue de Moussy, 4ᵉ, T 4272 1919

Patrick Seguin

This voluminous, beautifully lit gallery, owned by Patrick and Laurence Seguin and remodelled in 2003 by Jean Nouvel, is the home of furnishings and decorative pieces by France's most important midcentury architects and designers. A typical exhibition will feature tables, chairs, shelves, shutters and ceramics by perennial Paris favourites Jean Prouvé and Charlotte Perriand, and also pieces by Le Corbusier, Pierre Jeanneret, Georges Jouve, Jean Royère and Serge Mouille. If you're shopping properly, your pockets will need to be well lined – rare items don't come cheap. However, if you are pretend shopping, you will leave this heavenly store with your imaginary modernist mansion fully furnished. *5 rue des Taillandiers, 11e, T 4700 3235, patrickseguin.com*

Comptoir de l'Image

Plenty of places claim to have famous
designers drop in on them, but John
Galliano and Marc Jacobs do regularly
come to this little gem of a shop in the
Marais, to stock up on old copies of
heritage glossies. It's the Parisian answer
to the fashionista hangout Gallagher's
in New York, whose walk-in store has
now sadly closed (call 212 473 2404 for
emergency magazine requests). As
well as vintage fashion titles, from *Vogue*
and *Harper's Bazaar* to *The Face* and
everything else in-between, Comptoir
de l'Image stocks a catholic range of
contemporary magazines, including
Purple and *Spoon*. In a sense, this shop
could be described as an ideas vault.
Although it's tiny, it is also packed with
a splendid collection of photography and
design books. Browse, enjoy, plagiarise.
44 rue de Sévigné, 3ᵉ, T 4272 0392

Givenchy

Creative director Riccardo Tisci selected London-based architect Jamie Fobert to design Givenchy's store on rue du Faubourg Saint-Honoré, which opened its doors in February 2008. Better known for his exhibition spaces for the Tate and Frieze Art Fair, Fobert's space feels more like a gallery, thanks to the white walls and oak parquet flooring. The principal design element, five room-sized boxes, houses the ready-to-wear. The boxes are constructed in burnt oak, encased in layers of resin, and the interior of each offers a variation on a classical theme, from baroque-style panelling with moulding embossed into leather, to art deco-like glass panelling and grey plaster basalt with parquet for the menswear.
*28 rue du Faubourg Saint-Honoré, 8ᵉ,
T 4268 3100, givenchy.com*

Maison Darré

This surrealist cabinet of curiosities is full of tables with aluminium legs shaped like femur bones and lamps like human skulls with spectacles. It's the dream project of Vincent Darré, a former fashion designer for Fendi, Moschino and Ungaro. The items are by him or his designer friends, such as Marie Brandolini, and crafted as limited editions. Future offerings include erotic wallpaper by French actress Valerie Lemercier. Darré's design influences include Dalí and Dada, and his passion for bones was inspired by a strictly atheist upbringing combined with a love of Italy, where Christian relics abound. This intimate space resembles a chapel of the absurd, its creations not just anatomically inspired but also totally tongue-in-cheek. *32 rue du Mont Thabor, 1er, T 4260 2797, maisondarre.com*

The Different Company

This *haute parfumerie* boasts an impressive pedigree. Its principal perfumer, Céline Ellena, is the daughter of Jean-Claude Ellena, current head nose at Hermès and creator of the Eau Parfumée au Thé Vert for Bulgari, and the flacons and flagship store here in the Marais were created by Jean-Claude's cousin, esteemed bottle designer Thierry de Baschmakoff. The lacquered white walls and shelving create a sleek space in which The Different Company's loyal clientele sample its perfumes, sniffing the scents first from a wine glass. Ellena aims to create a new fragrance each year. Sublime Balkiss, released in 2008, with its notes of violet and patchouli, has proved a bestseller, though we're also fans of the sweet/salty Sel de Vétiver. Oriental Lounge is her 2009 creation. Most bottles are refillable.
10 rue Ferdinand Duval, 4ᵉ, T 4278 1934, thedifferentcompany.com

SPORTS AND SPAS

WORK OUT, CHILL OUT OR JUST WATCH

In the popular imagination and, it should be said, to a very great extent in reality, Paris is not a sporting town. Its gyms are dotted with the broken bodies of visitors who had imagined that the machinery was there to be used and not just to provide a backdrop, a kind of modern art installation, behind a cool juice bar. However, this is changing. Joggers can now be spotted in the Jardin du Luxembourg, some of them in serious training for the Paris Marathon (parismarathon.com). Held every April, this is very nearly worth the pain because of its stunning route, beginning at the Arc de Triomphe. Even so, it is an event that most Parisians prefer to watch rather than take part in. And, as a spectator sport, it pales into insignificance compared to the epicurean pleasures to be enjoyed at the Grand Prix de Saint-Cloud and Grand Prix de l'Arc de Triomphe – the twin pillars of Parisian horse racing.

The biggest crowds of all are reserved for the third week in July, when the final stage of the Tour de France (letour.fr) races through Paris, before the final sprint on the Champs-Élysées. For weeks before, the streets are full of amateurs emulating their heroes. For those who prefer *la natation*, the Piscine Pontoise-Quartier Latin (19 rue de Pontoise, 5e, T 5542 7788) is a 33m glass-roofed art deco pool that plays underwater music for night-time swimmers. And, of course, Paris boasts the chicest spas imaginable. *For full addresses, see Resources.*

Dior Institut

In 1946, the fashion designer Christian Dior opened a boutique near the Hotel Plaza Athénée (see p028) on avenue Montaigne. The location turned out to be rather well chosen. The Plaza has long been one of Paris's most fashionable venues and, in 2008, it launched the Dior Institut, offering beauty treatments for men and women. The grey and white mirrored spa, designed by Patrick Ribes, has flatscreens showing recent Dior collections on the entrance walls, and contains five treatment rooms, including a VIP room for two, a fitness centre, relaxation lounge, sauna and hammam area. Its signature treatment, L'Or de Vie, is a reviver *par excellence* created in collaboration with Château d'Yquem.
25 avenue Montaigne, 8ᵉ, T 5367 6535, www.plaza-athenee-paris.com

La Maison Guerlain
In 2005, architect Maxime d'Angeac and designer Andrée Putman reinvigorated what had been the world's first modern beauty institute when it opened in 1939. In a flurry of golden mosaic tiles and glass beads, the pair transformed the first floor into a scent emporium (pictured) and the second into a spa.
68 avenue des Champs-Élysées, 8ᵉ, T 4562 1121, guerlain.com

L'Appartement 217

This impressive seven-room temple to wellbeing is the creation of Stéphane Jaulin, whose sound grounding in beauty came from a stint at Guerlain (see p090) and as manager of the cosmetics section at Colette (T 5535 3390). It was also the first wholly organic pamper-palace in the city, with a resolutely holistic approach taken towards the interior and the products, which include Senteurs de Feé and Jaulin's own line, Stéphane Jaulin Cosmetics. Treatments offered here are both high- and low-tech, from a superlative facial, €170 (one-and-a-half hours), to a session in the Japanese 'Iyashi Dôme', €60 (one hour), a ceramic chamber that uses heat to help eliminate toxins – and, hopefully, a few calories.
217 rue Saint-Honoré, 1er, T 4296 0096, lappartement217.com

Anne Fontaine Spa

Brazilian-French designer Anne Fontaine opened this spa in the basement of her rue Saint-Honoré boutique in 2007. Designed in collaboration with Andrée Putman, the space subtly combines urban and organic elements to reflect Fontaine's fashion ethos. The flooring is comprised of parquet, grey stone and white resin, and the combination of wood, stone and water gives the impression of entering an urban grotto. The treatments take their cue from the natural materials that the designer uses for her clothing, and include massages with cotton oil, silk-fibre cream and bamboo shoots. The products used are part of two lines that Fontaine launched for the spa, called Natural Linen and Silk Performance.
370 rue Saint-Honoré, 1er, T 4261 0370, annefontaine.com

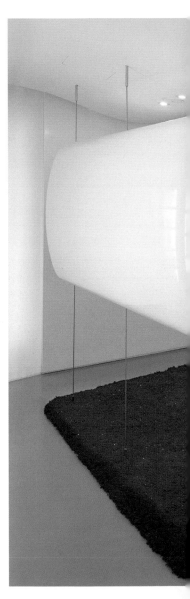

La Bulle Kenzo
Only a sauna and plunge pool short of
a traditional spa set-up, La Bulle, situated
on the fourth floor of the arresting Kenzo
building on rue du Pont Neuf, nevertheless
meets the essential requirements of a
contemporary urban retreat – exceptional
treatments with exquisite products, served
up in an extraordinary environment.
The striking treatment pods, designed by
Emmanuelle Duplay, may look like they
harbour the nerve centre of an alien
invasion but, in fact, they offer beautifully
lit havens. One is designed for relaxation
(matt flooring, wooden details and a film
projection of wafting plants), another for
euphoria (golden mosaic tiles, glass pearls
and a 'hairy' outer shell). Opt for the
Massage Guimauve (face, hands and feet)
or the Massage au Chandelles et aux Riz,
a gentle pummelling with rice grains.
1 rue du Pont Neuf, , T 4236 5673,
labullekenzo.com

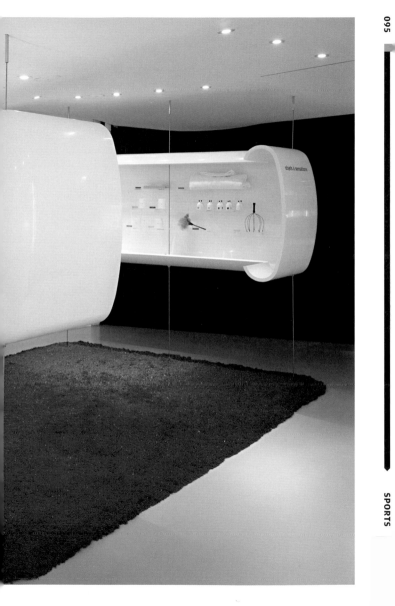

ESCAPES

WHERE TO GO IF YOU WANT TO LEAVE TOWN

Even today, when most travel has become so commodified, there is still something impossibly glamorous about the destination boards at Parisian railway stations, burnished, as they are, with the names of Europe's most beautiful cities. There can be surely no better way of preparing to leave Paris than by lingering over *un allongé* in the wonderfully overblown rococo of Le Train Bleu dining room at the Gare de Lyon (place Louis Armand, 12e, T 4343 0906), before boarding a sleeper train to the south and the sun.

The improved scope of the TGV network means that you can get to Le Havre for an Auguste Perret architour in just over two hours, or to Deauville for seafood and sandy beaches in about the same time. Closer to home, the MAC/VAL museum (see p100), located in luxuriant parkland in the south-eastern suburb of Vitry-sur-Seine, makes for a pleasant half-day diversion, but can take almost as long to get to by decidedly unglamorous local train and bus. Le Pré Catelan restaurant (route de Suresnes, 16e, T 4414 4114), in the Bois de Boulogne, isn't strictly a day trip, but it is a lovely place to lose an afternoon. In Poissy, to the north-west, there is Villa Savoye (see p102), the most celebrated modernist house. Further afield, in the proper countryside of Champagne, about 90 minutes away by car (45 minutes by train from Gare d'Est), is Les Crayères (opposite), a perfect country escape with a sensational restaurant. *For full addresses, see Resources.*

Les Crayères, Reims

Nestled in a park full of grand old chestnut trees, this picturesque château (overleaf) is home to one of France's best gourmet escapes. There are a total of 20 rooms, 17 of which are located in the château itself, such as the Princess Room (above), with a further three in a nearby cottage. There's no denying the fact that there is a certain amount of chintz on display here at all times (it seems inevitable that Miss Marple will emerge from the drawing room at some stage), but, overall, the design isn't too fussy for what is a supremely elegant destination. Le Parc restaurant, which has two Michelin stars, is the main draw for many guests. There is also now a brasserie, Le Jardin, which opened in May 2009.

64 boulevard Henry Vasnier,
T 03 2682 8080, www.lescrayeres.com

MAC/VAL, Vitry-sur-Seine
This gallery is the only reason to visit
the suburb of Vitry-sur-Seine, but it is
a compelling one. All horizontal lines
and glass walls, Jacques Ripault's 2005
building displays a well curated collection
of mostly French art from the past 60
years, including works by Valérie Jouve,
Christian Boltanski and Delphine Coindet.
*Place de la Libération, T 4391 6420,
macval.fr*

Villa Savoye, Poissy
Le Corbusier conceived the glamorous
Villa Savoye, the purest of his purist
villas, as a 'box in the air'. He used the
house's structure to orchestrate the
experience of entering it, as if he were
directing a film. Situated in a field of
straggling daisies, it was completed
in 1931. Don't miss it. Closed Mondays.
82 rue de Villiers, T 3965 0106,
villa-savoye.monuments-nationaux.fr

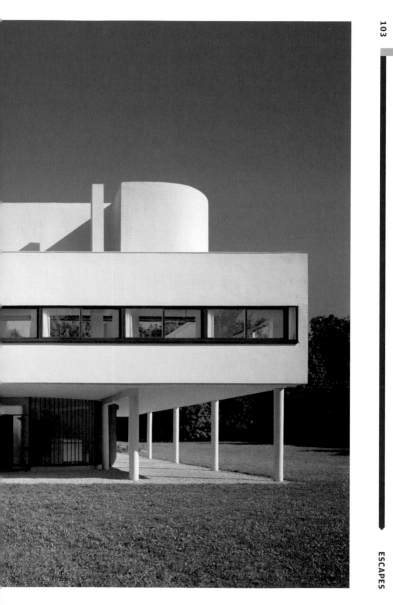

NOTES
SKETCHES AND MEMOS

RESOURCES

CITY GUIDE DIRECTORY

HOTELS

ADDRESSES AND ROOM RATES

Hôtel Le A 026
Room rates:
double, from €200;
Junior Suite 402, from €275
4 rue d'Artois, 8ᵉ
T 4256 9999
paris-hotel-a.com

Le Bellechasse 029
Room rates:
double, from €260;
Quai d'Orsay Room, from €260
8 rue de Bellechasse, 7ᵉ
T 4550 2231
lebellechasse.com

Les Crayères 097
Room rates:
double, from €325;
Princess Room, from €540
64 boulevard Henry Vasnier
Reims
T 03 2682 8080
lescrayeres.com

Hôtel Fouquet's Barrière 016
Room rates:
double, from €590
46 avenue George V/
avenue des Champs-Élysées, 8ᵉ
T 4069 6000
fouquets-barriere.com

L'Hôtel 027
Room rates:
double, from €345;
Rooms 16 and 36, from €540
13 rue des Beaux Arts, 6ᵉ
T 4441 9900
l-hotel.com

Mama Shelter 023
Room rates:
double, from €90;
Mama Luxe Room, €109
109 rue de Bagnolet, 20ᵉ
T 4348 4848
mamashelter.com

Le Meurice 016
Room rates:
double, from €520
228 rue de Rivoli, 1ᵉʳ
T 4458 1010
lemeurice.com

9 Hotel 022
Room rates:
double, from €110;
Superior Room, from €260
14 rue Papillon, 9ᵉ
T 4770 7834
le9hotel.com

Hôtel Particulier 017
Room rates:
double, €390;
Curtain of Hair Suite, from €590
23 avenue Junot, 18ᵉ
T 5341 8140
hotel-particulier-montmartre.com

Hôtel du Petit Moulin 020
Room rates:
double, from €190;
Room 204, €290
29-31 rue du Poitou, 3ᵉ
T 4274 1010
paris-hotel-petitmoulin.com

Hôtel Plaza Athénée 028
  Room rates:
  double, from €740;
  Deluxe Room, from €860;
  Royal Suite, €20,000
  25 avenue Montaigne, 8^e
  T 5367 6665
  www.plaza-athenee-paris.com
Le Royal Monceau 016
  Room rates:
  prices on request
  37 avenue Hoche, 8^e
  T 4299 8800
  www.royalmonceau.com
3 Rooms 030
  Room rates:
  double, €450
  7 rue de Moussy, 4^e
  T 4478 9200
  www.3rooms-10corsocomo.com

WALLPAPER* CITY GUIDES

Editorial Director
Richard Cook

Art Director
Loran Stosskopf
Editor
Rachael Moloney
Authors
Sara Henrichs
Paul McCann
Deputy Editor
Jeremy Case
Managing Editor
Jessica Diamond

Chief Designer
Daniel Shrimpton
Designers
Benjamin Blossom
Lara Collins
Map Illustrator
Russell Bell

Photography Editor
Sophie Corben
Photography Assistant
Robin Key

Sub-Editor
Stephen Patience
Editorial Assistant
Ella Marshall

Interns
Jane Duru
Tiffany Jow

**Wallpaper* Group
Editor-in-Chief**
Tony Chambers
Publishing Director
Gord Ray

Contributors
Emma Blau
Trish Deseine
Marie Lefort
Amy Serafin
Nick Vinson

Wallpaper* ® is a
registered trademark
of IPC Media Limited

All prices are correct at
time of going to press,
but are subject to change.

Printed in China

PHAIDON

Phaidon Press Limited
Regent's Wharf
All Saints Street
London N1 9PA

Phaidon Press Inc
180 Varick Street
New York, NY 10014

Phaidon® is a registered
trademark of Phaidon
Press Limited

www.phaidon.com

First published 2006
Second edition (revised
and updated) 2008
Third edition (revised
and updated) 2009
© 2006, 2008 and 2009
IPC Media Limited

ISBN 978 0 7148 5641 4

A CIP Catalogue record for
this book is available from
the British Library.

PHOTOGRAPHERS

Gerard Bedeau
L'Atelier de Joël
Robuchon, p054

Thomas Brodin
Grande Arche de la
Défense, p010
UNESCO
Headquarters, p012
Basilique du
Sacré-Coeur, p013
Benoit, p048
Cité de Refuge, p065
Maison du Brésil, p068
Maison de Verre, p069
Villa Savoye, pp102-103

Corbis
Paris city view,
inside front cover

Morgane Le Gall
Galerie Kreo, p036

Jaques Gavard
Gaya Rive Gauche,
pp044-045

Alexandre Guirkinger
Merci, p037
The Ritz Bar, p058
Comptoir de l'Image,
pp082-083
Alex Hill
Hôtel Particulier, p017,
pp018-019
Mama Shelter, p023
Musée du Quai Branly,
pp034-035
La Société, pp038-039
Unico, p041
Le Cochon à l'Oreille,
pp050-051
Paris Social Club,
pp060-061
Vanessa and Laetitia
Roggwiller, p063
Pierre Hardy, pp074-075
Hôtel Particulier,
p078, p079
Maison Darré, p085
The Different Company,
pp086-087

**Jean-Noel
Leblanc-Bontemps**
Sanofi-Aventis building,
pp066-067
Boulogne-Billancourt,
pp070-071
La Maison Guerlain,
pp090-091

**Courtesy of Patrick
Seguin Gallery**
Patrick Seguin, p081

Philippe Schaff
Apicius, p055

Pauline Turmel
MAC/VAL, pp100-101

PARIS

A COLOUR-CODED GUIDE TO THE CITY'S HOT 'HOODS

MONTMARTRE
Up the hill is home to the *haute bourgeoisie*; at its foot is the city's (reformed) sin central

SAINT-MARTIN
It's by this canal in the 10ᵉ arrondissement that the east Paris bobo set shop and play

GRANDS BOULEVARDS
Les Champs will always be touristy, but the area around it is full of stylish destinations

RÉPUBLIQUE AND BASTILLE
More polished these days, thanks to a shot of *bon chic, bon genre*. Eat on rue Paul Bert

MARAIS
These streets were made for strolling. Galleries, boutiques, bars and bistros, it's all here

LOUVRE AND BEAUBOURG
Art collections and architecture that are impossible to miss and still able to surprise

SAINT-GERMAIN AND QUARTIER LATIN
Sartre and de Beauvoir's Left Bank stomping ground is more about shopping these days

LES INVALIDES
The monumental heart of the city now has another prize – Jean Nouvel's museum

For a full description of each neighbourhood, see the Introduction.
Featured venues are colour-coded, according to the district in which they are located.